FOLLOW THE
PROMPTS, SCRATCH
OFF THE PANELS,
RECORD YOUR
THOUGHTS AND
DISCOVER 50 WAYS
TO FIND YOUR
TRUE SELF

-
-
-
-
-
-
-
-
-

"KNOWING OTHERS IS WISDOM, KNOWING YOURSELF IS ENLIGHTENMENT"

LAOZI

STAND IN FRONT OF THE MIRROR FOR TWO MINUTES

WHO DO YOU SEE?

" THE WORST OF ALL DECEPTIONS IS SELF-DECEPTION "

PLATO

"I AM MINE BEFORE I AM EVER ANYONE ELSE'S"

NAYYIRAH WAHEED

LIFE'S A JOURNEY

HOW'S THE JOURNEY SO FAR?
WHAT HAVE BEEN THE HIGHLIGHTS?

1.

2.

3.

WHERE WOULD YOU LIKE TO GO NEXT ON THE JOURNEY OF LIFE?

1.

2.

3.

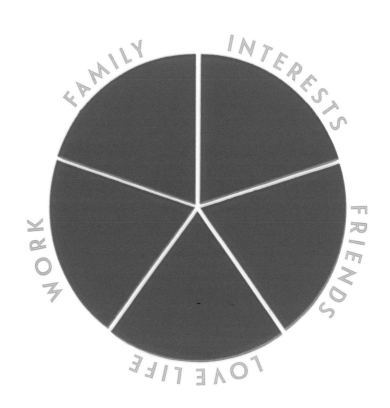

FAMILY
INTERESTS
FRIENDS
LOVE LIFE
WORK

SCRATCH OFF THE SEGMENTS
THAT MEAN MOST TO YOU

WHICH OF THESE ELEMENTS MOST
CONTRIBUTES TO YOUR SENSE OF IDENTITY?

HOW WOULD ██████ DESCRIBE YOURSELF IN THREE WORDS?

1

2

3

HOW WOULD YOUR █████████ DESCRIBE YOU IN THREE WORDS?

1

2

3

HOW WOULD YOUR ████████ DESCRIBE YOU IN THREE WORDS?

1

2

3

HOW WOULD YOUR ████████ DESCRIBE YOU IN THREE WORDS?

1

2

3

WHO KNOWS YOU BEST?

1 REMEMBER HOW YOU WERE LAST YEAR

2 CONSIDER HOW YOU HAVE CHANGED SO·FAR THIS YEAR

CIRCLE THE WORDS YOU RECOGNISE IN YOURSELF

KIND	BRISK
SNAPPY	SECRETIVE
RESILIENT	HONEST
COURAGEOUS	PLAYFUL
IDLE	SELF-DISCIPLINED
CONFIDENT	NARCISSISTIC

WHICH OTHER WORDS WOULD YOU USE TO DESCRIBE YOURSELF? (TELL THE TRUTH!)

WRITE DOWN THREE WORDS YOU WOULD LIKE OTHERS TO USE TO DESCRIBE YOU

1 _____

2 _____

3 _____

SELF
PERCEPTION

100%

WRITE YOUR CHOSEN
WORDS BENEATH EACH
BAR AND SCRATCH OFF
THE PERCENTAGE OF
EACH DESCRIPTION YOU
ALREADY EMBODY

HOW CAN YOU IMPROVE
YOUR SCORE?

0%

LIST THE CHARACTERISTICS YOU ADMIRE IN OTHERS
HOW MANY DO YOU SHARE?

DO YOU WANT TO BE...

DRAW THE ANIMAL WITH WHICH
YOU MOST IDENTIFY

WHICH CELEBRITIES DO YOU LOOK UP TO?

WHO DO YOU ADMIRE IN REAL LIFE?

HAS ANYONE,
KNOWN OR
UNKNOWN,
EVER...

HAVE YOU EVER...

"YOU ARE NEVER TOO OLD TO SET ANOTHER GOAL OR TO DREAM A NEW DREAM"

C.S. LEWIS

WHAT DO YOU

"THE GREAT MAN IS HE WHO DOES NOT LOSE HIS CHILD'S HEART"

MENG-TZU

WHAT WERE YOU LIKE AS A CHILD?

WHAT WERE YOU LIKE AS A TEENAGER?

SCRATCH YOUR SELF-PORTRAIT

WHAT MAKES YOU ...

WRITE DOWN THE LAST FIVE TIMES YOU FELT JOY

1.

2.

3.

4.

5.

WHAT ARE YOU MOST ███████ ABOUT?

_____

_____

_____

_____

_____

WHAT ARE THE BEST THINGS ABOUT YOUR ████?

_____

_____

_____

ARE YOU HAPPIEST AROUND ███████ OR ███████████

WHEN DO YOU FEEL MOST ██████████

HOW DO YOU FEEL?

SCRATCH OFF
WHAT PERCENTAGE
OF EACH EMOTION
YOU FELT TODAY

100%

0%

OVER THE MOON

ONLY OKAY

LIFE'S A DRAG

"HAPPINESS IS
WHEN WHAT YOU
THINK, WHAT YOU
SAY AND WHAT
YOU DO ARE IN
HARMONY"

GHANDI

SCRATCH OFF THE RELEVANT NUMBER OF BOXES NEXT TO THE FOLLOWING QUESTIONS

TODAY, HOW MANY PEOPLE HAVE YOU:

MADE LAUGH

CALLED FOR A CHAT

HELPED OUT

SURPRISED

MADE PROUD

THANKED

CARED FOR

"HOME IS WHERE ONE STARTS FROM"

T.S. ELIOT

WHERE ON EARTH ARE YOU HAPPIEST?
SKETCH OR WRITE IT OUT

IF YOU WON THE LOTTERY WHO WOULD YOU GIVE THE MONEY TO?

I'D KEEP IT ALL MYSELF ☐

I'D SHARE IT WITH FAMILY AND FRIENDS ☐

I'D SHARE IT WITH FAMILY, FRIENDS, MYSELF AND CHARITY ☐

I'D GIVE IT ALL AWAY

"A LITTLE THOUGHT AND A LITTLE KINDNESS ARE WORTH MORE THAN A GREAT DEAL OF MONEY"

JOHN RUSKIN

WHAT MAKES
YOU...

WRITE DOWN YOUR MOST EMBARRASSING CHARACTERISTICS

HAVE YOU EVER ▮▮▮▮▮▮ ANYTHING?

_____

_____

_____

_____

WHAT HAVE YOU ▮▮▮▮▮▮ ON?

_____

_____

_____

_____

WHEN WAS THE LAST TIME YOU ████████████ ██████████

_____

_____

_____

_____

HAVE YOU EVER ████████████████

_____

_____

_____

_____

WHAT MAKES
YOU ...

CLOSE YOUR EYES AND VISUALISE YOUR GREATEST FEAR

"YOUR SOUL
IS A DARK FOREST"

MARCEL PROUST

WHAT MAKES YOU ...

GO ON - REALLY LET RIP!

RUDENESS

IMPATIENCE

CASUALNESS

CYNICISM

PESSIMISM

LAZINESS

NEUROTICISM

UNPREDICTABILITY

STUBBORNNESS

HYPERSENSITIVITY

LATENESS

MOODINESS

HOW MANY OF THESE CHARACTERISTICS
DO YOU SHARE?

SCRATCH OUT THE RELEVANT NUMBER OF BOXES NEXT TO THE FOLLOWING QUESTIONS

TODAY, HOW MANY PEOPLE HAVE YOU:

MADE CRINGE

INFURIATED

MADE CRY

EMBARRASSED

SHOUTED AT

LET DOWN

IGNORED

"NOBODY HOLDS A GOOD OPINION OF A MAN WHO HAS A LOW OPINION OF HIMSELF"

ANTHONY TROLLOPE

WHAT IS YOUR VICE?

Scratch off the boxes and see if you could also
be attracted to the opposite virtue

LUST

SPENDING

GREED

SLOTH

WRATH

ENVY

PRIDE

VANITY

WHAT DO YOU LIKE BEST ABOUT YOURSELF?

"I LEARNED A LONG TIME AGO THE WISEST THING I CAN DO IS BE ON MY OWN SIDE, BE AN ADVOCATE FOR MYSELF"

MAYA ANGELOU

ALL CHARACTERISTICS
CAN BE IMPROVED

Controlling   ——→

Stubborn   ——→

Boring   ——→

Secretive   ——→

Snappy   ——→

Idle   ——→

Narcisstic   ——→

YOUR GOALS SHOULD BE

S
M
A
R
T

WRITE DOWN YOUR FUTURE GOALS

MAKE YOUR OWN STANDARDS

ON SOCIAL MEDIA

I WILL

_____

_____

_____

I WILL NOT

_____

_____

_____

AT WORK

I WILL

_____

_____

_____

I WILL NOT

_____

_____

_____

WITH MY PARTNER

I WILL

_____

_____

_____

I WILL NOT

_____

_____

_____

WITH MY FRIENDS & FAMILY

I WILL

_____

_____

_____

I WILL NOT

_____

_____

_____

WHERE DO YOU
WANT TO BE IN

ONE

FIVE

TEN

"YOUR TIME IS LIMITED, SO DON'T WASTE IT LIVING SOMEONE ELSE'S LIFE...

HAVE THE COURAGE TO FOLLOW YOUR HEART AND INTUITION"

STEVE JOBS

BENEFITS OF BEING
YOUR TRUE SELF

MORE ▭

LESS ▭

A FEELING OF ▭

"THIS ABOVE ALL: TO THINE OWN SELF BE TRUE"

WILLIAM SHAKESPEARE

SCRATCH OFF LINES
MAKE LETTERS
SPELL OUT WORDS THAT REFLECT YOU

"AND REMEMBER, NO MATTER WHERE YOU GO, THERE YOU ARE"

CONFUCIUS

NICE TO
MEET YOU
LET'S CATCH
UP AGAIN
SOON